Dear Parent:
Your child's love of reading starts here!

Every child learns to read in a different way and at his or her own speed. Some go back and forth between reading levels and read favourite books again and again. Others read through each level in order. You can help your young reader improve and become more confident by encouraging his or her own interests and abilities. From books your child reads with you to the first books he or she reads alone, there are I Can Read Books for every stage of reading:

SHARED READING
Basic language, word repetition, and whimsical illustrations, ideal for sharing with your emergent reader

BEGINNING READING
Short sentences, familiar words, and simple concepts for children eager to read on their own

READING WITH HELP
Engaging stories, longer sentences, and language play for developing readers

READING ALONE
Complex plots, challenging vocabulary, and high-interest topics for the independent reader

ADVANCED READING
Short paragraphs, chapters, and exciting themes for the perfect bridge to chapter books

I Can Read Books have introduced children to the joy of reading since 1957. Featuring award-winning authors and illustrators and a fabulous cast of beloved characters, I Can Read Books set the standard for beginning readers.

A lifetime of discovery begins wi   magical words   Read!"

Visit www.icanre
on enriching your c

D0967494

HOCKEY

AT HOME

by Meg Braithwaite

Illustrations by Nick Craine

Collins

Mario Lemieux is a big hockey star.

He has won the Stanley Cup
five times.

He has played hockey everywhere.

When Mario was a kid,

he didn't just play table hockey.

He didn't just watch hockey on TV.

He didn't just play hockey

at the rink.

What Mario did was
much more magical.

Mario's family loved hockey.

Papa loved it.

His brothers loved it.

Maybe Mama loved it most of all.

In the winter,

Papa built a rink on the front lawn.

Mario and his brothers skated on it.

They loved playing hockey on it too.

One day it was snowing very hard.

The snow covered the rink.

It was very deep.

Papa tried to clear off the ice.

Mario and his brothers helped.

But it didn't work.

"It's snowing too fast," said Mario.

Papa and the boys had to give up
and go inside.

Mario and his brothers opened
the front door.
They marched into the house.

The boys were covered in snow.
But they walked right into
the living room.

"Stop, stop," said Mama.

"Look at my carpet!"

Mario and his brothers looked down.

16

The carpet was covered in snow.
The snow was melting and
making wet spots.

Mario and his brothers

felt bad about the carpet.

But they were also sad.

"We want to play hockey," they said.

Mama looked at the snowy carpet.

"I have an idea," she said.

"But I'll need your help."

First, Mama turned off the heat.

Then she opened the windows.

Gusts of air filled the house.

"We have to get this place cold,"

Mama said.

Next, she opened the front door.

"And now for the snow!" Mama said.

Mama went out to the yard.

She came back with

a shovel full of snow.

Mama carried the snow

to the living room.

She dumped it on the carpet.

Mario and his brothers

couldn't believe it!

Mama brought in more snow.

And more snow.

And more.

Until the carpet was covered.

Then Mama used the shovel

to press the snow down.

She made the snow hard and even.

It was just like a sheet of ice.

The living room was a skating rink!

"Get your skates on!" Mama said.

Mario and his brothers played
hockey in their living room.

They skated past the sofa.

They passed the puck by the TV.

Later Mama would say,

"They really ruined my rug."

Not everyone believes the story.

But Mario remembers.

"It was the best hockey rink ever,"
Mario said.